Mr. TweeT's Mustache

By Charles S. Hellman & Robert A. Tiritilli

Mr. TweeT's Mustache

Copyright 2014

ALL RIGHT RESERVED
39844 Somerset Ave.
Palm Desert, CA 92211
www.LuckySports.net
(760) 861-2174

All rights reserved. Do not duplicate or redistribute in any form. All contents of this book including the concept, elements of design and layout, graphic images and elements, unless otherwise noted, is copyrighted material and protected by trade and other laws and may not be copied or imitated in whole or in part. Violators will be prosecuted to the maximum extent possible. No logo, graphic, character or caption from any page may be copied or retransmitted unless expressly permitted in writing by LuckySports$_{TM}$. Any rights not expressly granted herein are reserved.

ISBN 978-0-935938-60-9

Written & Illustrated by Robert A. Tiritilli

Cover & Interior Designed by Charles S. Hellman

Edited by Nila B. Hagood

"Hi there! Kicki is my name
and soccer is my game!
Striker's my big brother,
I wouldn't want any other."
"Striker and I are All Star greats,
And best of all, we're also TeamMates!"

"TeamMates!
That's the name of our team.
Our players are All Stars, really the cream.
Each one of the TeamMates excels in their game.
Can you tell which sport gave them such fame?"

**Kicki just returned from a wonderful week
in SportsLand's Soccer Camp, it was totally sweet.
She had learned some new moves for blocking and passing,
and Striker, she knew, would be sure to be asking.**

With the party they had at the end of the camp,
Kicki was feeling even more like a Champ!
She texted and tweeted to all of her friends,
talking of SportsLand, where the fun never ends.

**The TeamMates will soon play the big final big game
Against the bad Hoo-Doos, but it's really a shame.**

because they won't play nice and they don't play fair.
So root for the TeamMates and we'll see you there.

"We need to defend SportsLand.
There's a lot here at stake,
If the Hoo-Doos should win it, it's SportsLand they'll take."
Striker was urging his team to do well.
His TeamMates were with him, it was easy to tell.

**The TeamMates are fired up and ready to play.
When they last played the Hoo-Doos, Kicki saved the day.
She made a great shot at the last of the match,
One that their goalie just couldn't catch.**

"Though the Hoo-Doos are cheaters, we really don't care,
Our Ref, Mr. TweeT, will keep the game fair."
Mr. TweeT has this mustache, a glorious thing,
With ends all curled up and coiled like a spring.
Mr. TweeT has a habit of twirling his "stache"
as he watches the game and the players who clash.

If someone, indeed, commits a foul or acts bad,
a penalty card is held over their head.
Then he points at the player, who committed the deed,
and tweets on his whistle with incredible speed.

The big game should start now, the TeamMates are set;
but there isn't a sign of the Hoo-Doos just yet!
Now the fellow who calls out each move of the game
Is a raspy voiced expert with the perfect name.
Mike O'Phone taps his mike and speaks out.
(His voice is so strong, there's no need to shout.)
"Play well and play fair!" he says to the team,
"And show those ole Hoo-Doos what teamwork can mean!"

"We need Mr. TweeT to start off this game,"
Kicki was worried, and called out his name.

"Don't worry", soothed Striker, "He'll be here, you'll see. Mr. TweeT is, above all, a great referee."

A hush of silence washed over the crowd.
They all heard the shouting for it really was loud.
Sure enough the Hoo-Doos were coming to play,
With nasty Coach Trouble leading the way.
They shouted and yelled out in voices so brash,
the crowd simply parted and let them all pass.
"We are the Hoo-Doos and we will play rough,
and boy will we beat you, by more than enough!"

Striker turned and said "Man, is he rude!
Coach Trouble always has such a BAD ATTITUDE!"
The TeamMates weren't worried, but stood there quite proud.
The crowd began cheering, and the noise was so loud!

**A Hoo-Doo was calling Kicki bad names,
and sticking his tongue out, playing "Bad Bully" games.**

It turns out that Trouble had been up to his tricks,
Because being a bully seems to give him some kicks.
He'd snuck on TweeT, and quick as a flash
Had cut off the ends of poor TweeT's great mustache.

"Where is Mr. TweeT?
I am worried that he is OKAY."

Mike o' Phone shouted over the crowd,
"There's Mr. TweeT, oh my gosh what is wrong?
There are tears in his eyes, and he's usually so strong!"

Mr. TweeT looked so sad, but finally he said,
"Coach Trouble, that bully, cut off the ends
of my magical mustache, right where it bends."

**Mr. Tweet was so upset he hardly could speak,
"That Trouble is a bully, and he makes me feel weak;
and now, my poor mustache, I've nothing to tweak.
How can I possibly call this game fair?
When I reach for my mustache there's nothing but air!"**

"That dirty Trouble did this.
Woo-Hoo, Hoo-Dooers why can't you be Good-Dooers?
Now the TeamMates may lose and the Hoo-Doos might win!"

Coach Trouble then yelled, "Hey TweeT, it's no crime,
it's simply a PAYBACK, and we think it's time
to stop all your tweeting and hollering 'foul'.
The way you tweet us just makes me growl!"

**Okay all you Hoo-Doos, let's show them who's tough,
we know how to cheat and that's more then enough.
We'll prove we are stronger and smarter by far.
We'll beat those TeamMates and you'll all be stars!**

Coach Trouble, that rascal, with no respect for poor Mr. TweeT,
snapped his suspenders, knocking him off his feet.
Our ref Mr. TweeT just lay on the ground,
while the stars in his head kept swirling around.

"Oh dear, Mr. TweeT, will you be alright?"
Raquette was so worried for he looked such a fright.
"Trouble breeds trouble, but you shouldn't be down,
We think you are the best referee in this town!"

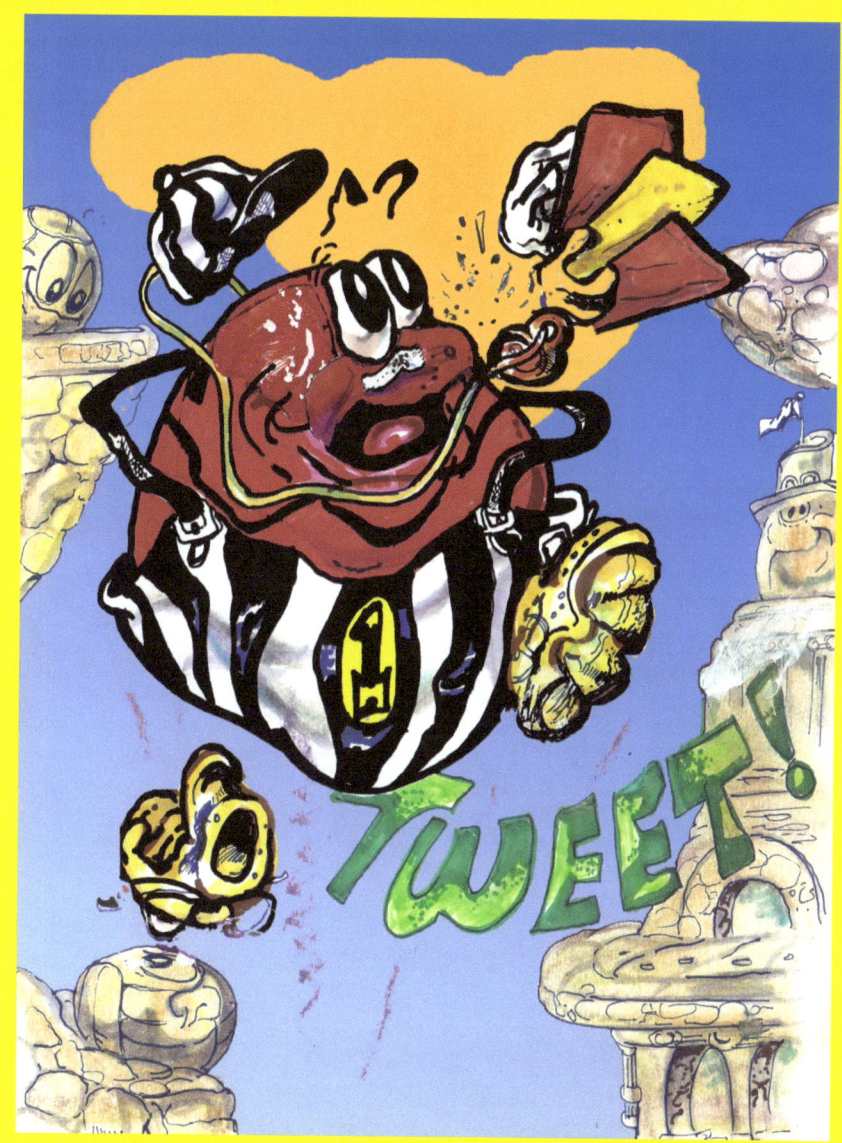

Mr. TweeT slowly rises, a little bit shaken
it was more than his mustache that Trouble had taken.
But he says, "I'm okay! That bully can't scare me!
I will do what I came for, Coach Trouble will see!"

Mr. TweeT lifts his whistle and tries a loud T-W-E-E-E-E-T
to signal the start of the game;
but nothing came out but a pitiful "phuweet"
(and boy! was it lame!).

"OH NO!" cried the TeamMates.
"His whistle won't work!"
Coach Trouble just watched and stifled his smirk.

"Come all you Hoo-Doos, there are no more rules!
Tripping, and handballs, bad thrown-ins are cool!
We will cheat every play, those TeamMates are fools,
Those Good-Dooers, the sissies, will sure lose this game,
the Hoo-Dooers will win and relish our fame!"

"Oh dear", cried Kicki, "what is there to do?
The Hoo-Doos will break all the good soccer rules!
With the Mr. TweeT's mustache in such disrepair
and his whistle not tweeting
This game won't be fair!"

"But, surely Mr. TweeT, you still can referee,
we are counting on you.
Think positive, you'll see!"

"All players on the field!
Let's have GOOD sportsmanship
from the beginning to the end."

With that Mr. Tweet shouted real loud
"The game is beginning," he said to the crowd.
No matter what happens
You play this game right,
and I'll see that you do, with all of my might."

When a team has a bad day,
The TeamMates all say, when you're in a pickle,
call for Coach Wiffle!

"Coach Wiffle! Coach Wiffle! We need your help fast!
The Hoo-Doos have cut off some of Mr. TweeT's great mustache!
Everything is all in great disarray,
The TeamMates need you to help save the day!

Those Hoo-Doos and Trouble are mean, nasty guys!
Look at what they've done, I'm NOT surprised.
Only the Hoo-Dooers would do what Hoo-Doos do
when the Hoo-Doos do what Hoo-Dooers do!
You must not delay, we've a big game to play."

**The Team began cheering, their spirits rose high
Coach Wiffle, they knew, was just the right guy.
"He is a Good-Dooer, he'll find the way
to make this mess better, and he'll save the day."**

**Trouble says,
"Wiffie, why bother coaching those who aren't fast or strong?"
Trouble continues taunting,
"The only reason to play any sport is to Win, Win, Win, Win,
not to play just for fun!"**

Those Hoo-Doos and Trouble are mean, nasty guys!
Look at what they've done, I'm NOT surprised.
Only the Hoo-Dooers would do what Hoo-Doos do
when the Hoo-Doos do what Hoo-Dooers do!
You must not delay, we've a big game to play."

"Hey!" said Coach Wiffle, I know what to do,
I just need Jolie the goalie to give me a curl or two.
Jolie the goalie has lots of hair,
let's go see if she has some to spare!
With a little bit of glue and tape,
we'll make sure that Mr. TweeT's stache gets back in shape!"

"I'm Joalie the goalie.
and I'm a Good-Dooer,
I have the hair if you have the glue!
A little bit here, and a little bit there,
give the ends a quick twist and
they'll point to the air!"

"Uh oh! The hair color, it's really all wrong, and Mr. Tweet's whistle still won't play it's song."

"You know I've been thinking,
though sometimes I'm slow,
and I've come up with something you should already know…"

We've ALL got something Hoo-Doos can't abide,
it's called POSITIVE ATTITUDE
and it comes from pride!"

Mr. TweeT touched a finger to the ends of his "stache", and it turned from orange to white in a flash!

"Yes," Mr. TweeT said, "I know it's for real!
and it's something no one, even Hoo-Doos, can steal!"

**The power of positive thinking really worked,
Mr. TweeT gave a great TWE-E-E-T,
Trouble turned with a jerk.**

"Look everyone!

Trouble and the Hoo-Doos are leaving,
grumbling and grunting because now they can't cheat.
That just shows they're quitters…
and quitters get beat!"

"It's like I always said,
even in the face of defeat,
cheaters never win,
and winner's NEVER cheat."

"Bye bye Hoo-Doos
We win again!"
Because we have pride and a good attitude,
and you really have nothing if you're a bully and rude.

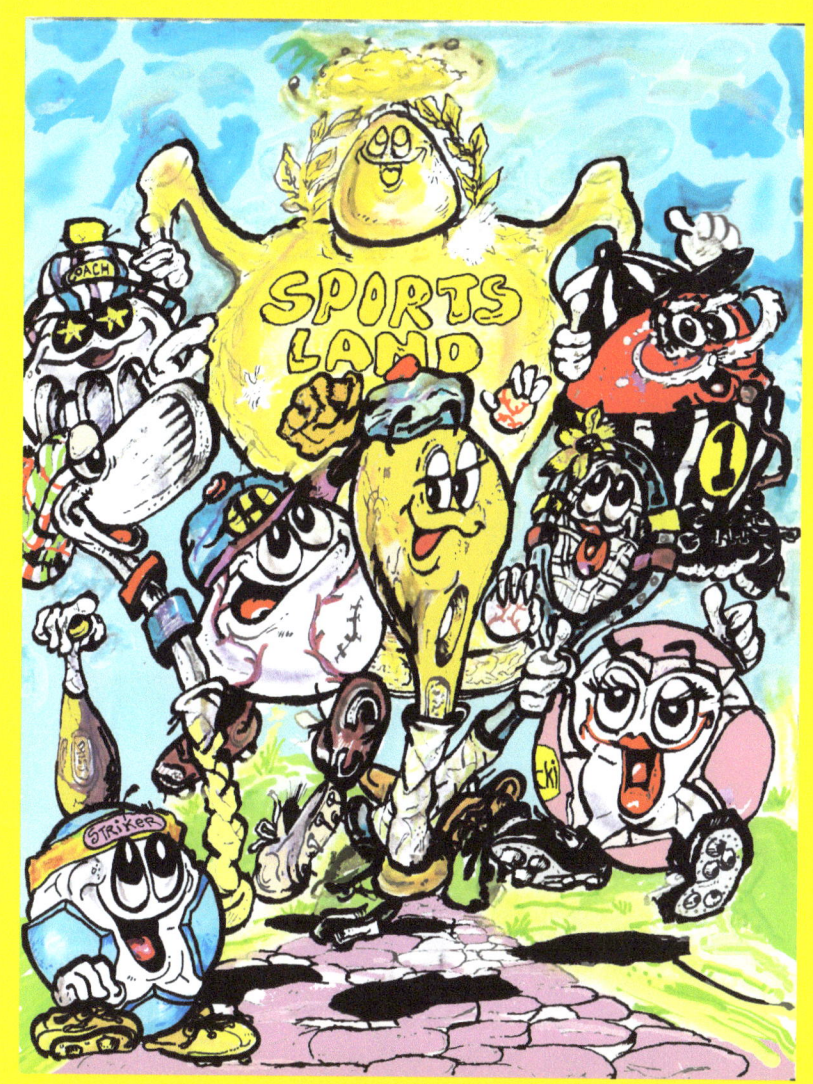

Go TeamMates, and hooray for Mr. Tweet!
And so we say goodbye to the team,
One and all they are Good-Dooers, and never are mean.
So be a good TeamMate and then
No matter what happens, you'll win in the end!

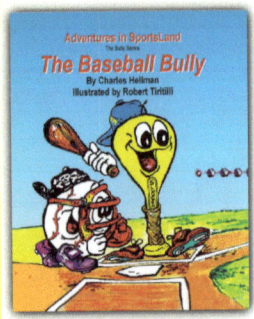

The Baseball Bully

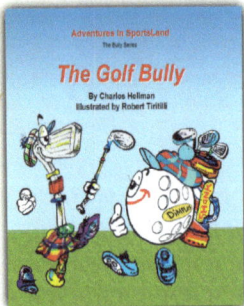

The Golf Bully

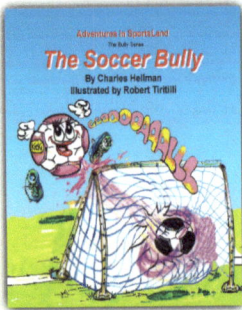

The Soccer Bully

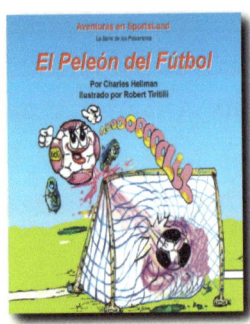

El Peleón del Fútbol

The Basketball Bully

One of the biggest problems a child faces today is BULLYING. Bullies are everywhere - in schools, on the internet, sports and playgrounds. Bully influence can affect and shape a young child's future views of life, especially in youth sports, where sports should be a fun and growing experience.

LuckySports has published ten titles of children's sports books from the *"Adventures in SportsLand"* Bully Series. These non-violent books subliminally teach children how to better understand the handling of bullies.

This bully series is aimed at children under 8 who are just beginning to interact with sport teams, coaches and players. These stories serve as an excellent tool for an adult to start a conversation with a child about bullies, good behavior and sportsmanship.

For more information see www.LuckySports.net All books are available for $8.95 on Amazon.com

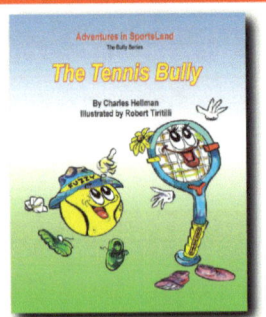

The Tennis Bully

The Football Bully

The Hockey Bully

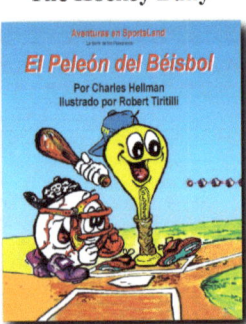

El Peleón del Béisbol

The Volleyball Bully

www.ingramcontent.com/pod-product-compliance
Lightning Source LLC
Chambersburg PA
CBHW042122040426
42450CB00002B/33